12/15

P9-BYQ-659

# ANDROMEDA

*Mary Austen*

**PowerKiDS** press™

New York

Published in 2016 by The Rosen Publishing Group, Inc.
29 East 21st Street, New York, NY 10010

First Edition

Editor: Katie Kawa
Book Design: Katelyn Heinle

Photo Credits: Cover, pp. 5, 11 (both) Yganko/Shutterstock.com; back cover, p. 1 nienora/Shutterstock.com; p. 7 angelinast/Shutterstock.com; p. 9 Science & Society Picture Library/SSPL/Getty Images; p. 10 Jurek Wyszynski/Photographer's Choice RF/Getty Images; p. 13 De Agostini/G. Dagli Orti/De Agostini Picture Library/Getty Images; p. 15 (main) Steven Puetzer/Photolibrary/Getty Images; p. 15 (inset) Rogelio Bernal Andreo/Stocktrek Images/Getty Images; p. 17 peresanz/Shutterstock.com; pp. 18, 19 Courtesy of NASA.gov; p. 21 MarcelClemens/Shutterstock.com; p. 22 © iStockphoto.com/YvanDube.

Library of Congress Cataloging-in-Publication Data

Austen, Mary, author.
 Andromeda / Mary Austen.
     pages cm. — (The constellation collection)
 Includes bibliographical references and index.
 ISBN 978-1-4994-0931-4 (pbk.)
 ISBN 978-1-4994-0951-2 (6 pack)
 ISBN 978-1-4994-0980-2 (library binding)
 1. Galaxies—Juvenile literature. 2. Constellations—Folklore—Juvenile literature. 3. Andromeda (Constellation)—Juvenile literature. 4. Andromeda Galaxy—Juvenile literature. I. Title.
 QB857.3.A97 2016
 523.1'12—dc23
                          2015000442

Manufactured in the United States of America

CPSIA Compliance Information: Batch #WS15PK: For Further Information contact Rosen Publishing, New York, New York at 1-800-237-9932

# CONTENTS

# A ROYAL CONSTELLATION

Groups of stars often form shapes. Thousands of years ago, people began mapping the outlines of people, animals, and objects they saw in groups of stars. These outlines were then given names. These named groups of stars are called constellations.

One group of constellations is named for a royal family from Greek **mythology**. The princess in this royal family was named Andromeda. The stars that make up her constellation form an A shape. A star that stands for Andromeda's head is at the point of the A shape. The rest of the stars make up her body.

## STAR STORY
Andromeda is one of 88 constellations that have been mapped in the sky and named.

SOME VERSIONS OF ANDROMEDA ARE MAPPED TO SHOW HER ARMS SPREAD OUT.

ANDROMEDA'S HEAD

# FINDING ANDROMEDA

You can find Andromeda in the sky by finding other stars that can lead you to this constellation. A popular way to find Andromeda is to look for a smaller group of stars, or asterism, called the Great Square of Pegasus. The Great Square of Pegasus is part of the larger Pegasus constellation.

The brightest star in the great square, Alpheratz, is also part of Andromeda. In fact, it's the constellation's point, or Andromeda's head. Andromeda can be seen in the Northern **Hemisphere** from June through February.

**STAR STORY**
Pegasus is the name of a flying horse in Greek mythology.

PEGASUS, SHOWN HERE, IS ONE CONSTELLATION YOU CAN USE TO HELP LOCATE, OR FIND, ANDROMEDA. LOOK FOR THE BRIGHTEST STAR IN THE GREAT SQUARE OF PEGASUS, AND YOU'VE FOUND ANDROMEDA'S HEAD.

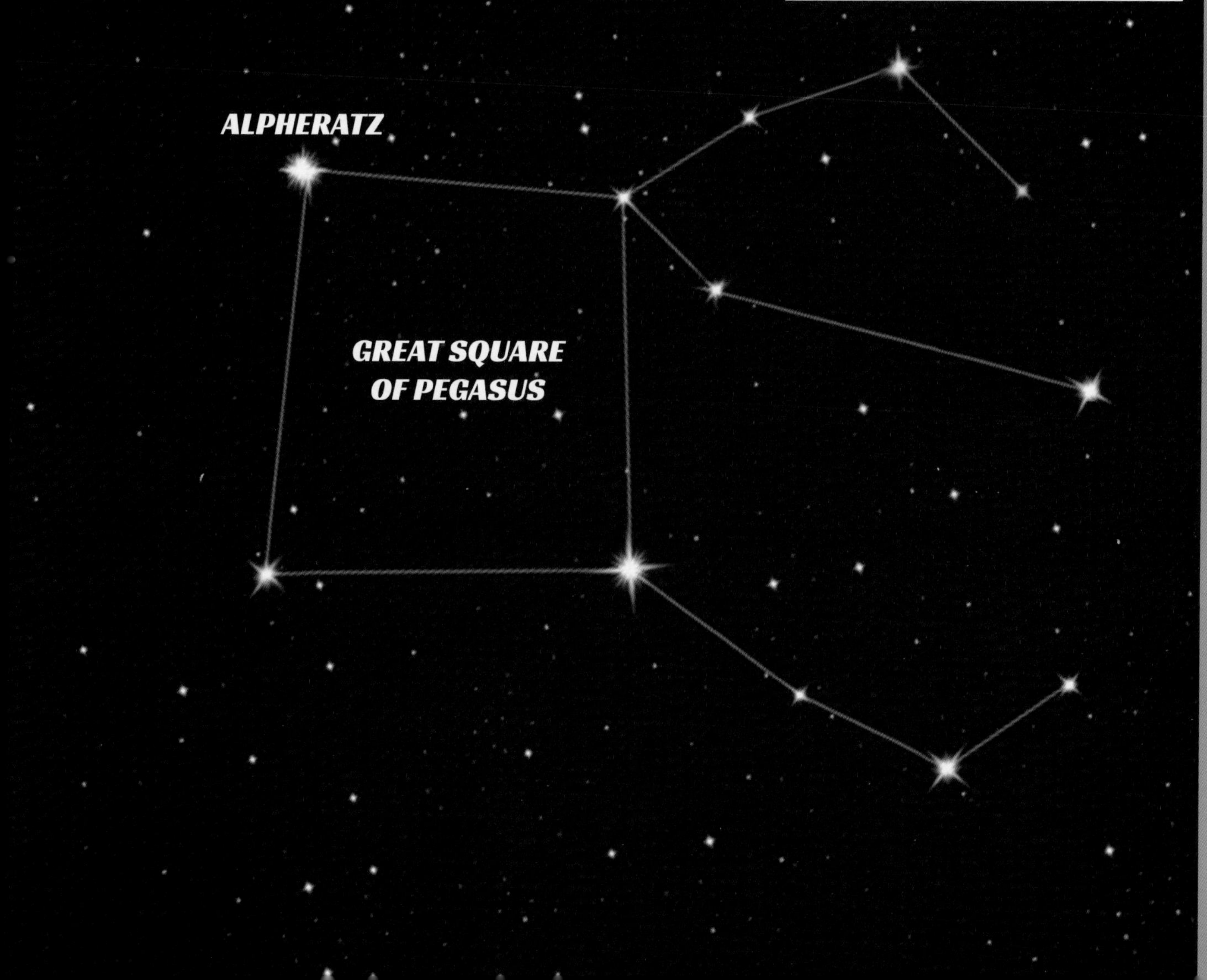

ALPHERATZ

GREAT SQUARE OF PEGASUS

# THE STORY OF ANDROMEDA

Andromeda, like many constellations, got its name from a person in ancient mythology. The ancient Greeks told the myth of Andromeda, who was the daughter of King Cepheus and Queen Cassiopeia. Cassiopeia bragged that Andromeda was more beautiful than the sea **nymphs**, which angered the sea god, Poseidon. Poseidon then sent a sea monster to attack Cepheus's kingdom.

Cepheus was told that he could save the kingdom by chaining Andromeda to a rock to be eaten by the sea monster. Andromeda was saved from this fate by Perseus, who then killed the sea monster. Andromeda and Perseus were later married.

## STAR STORY
The shapes of Andromeda and Perseus were believed to be in the stars because the goddess Athena placed them there after they died.

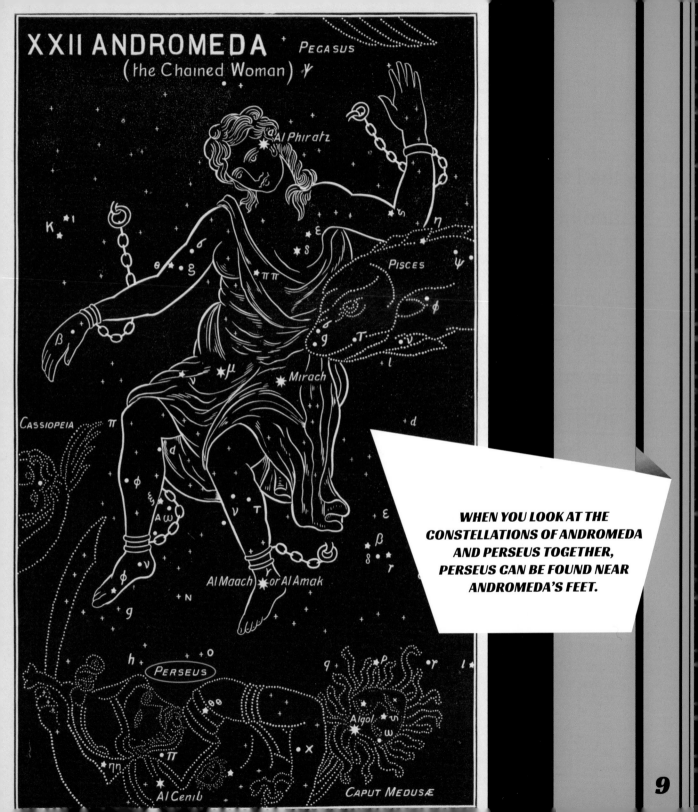

# XXII ANDROMEDA
## (the Chained Woman)

PEGASUS

Al Phiratz

PISCES

Mirach

CASSIOPEIA

Al Maach or Al Amak

WHEN YOU LOOK AT THE CONSTELLATIONS OF ANDROMEDA AND PERSEUS TOGETHER, PERSEUS CAN BE FOUND NEAR ANDROMEDA'S FEET.

PERSEUS

Algol

Al Cenib

CAPUT MEDUSÆ

# THE PERSEUS FAMILY

Andromeda is part of a group of constellations called the Perseus family. These constellations are near one another in the night sky, and many of them are named after people who were part of the same Greek myth. This family of constellations includes Andromeda, Cassiopeia, Cepheus, and Perseus. The Perseus family also includes the constellations of Pegasus, Cetus, Auriga, Lacerta, and Triangulum.

To find the Perseus family of constellations, first find Cassiopeia, which is shaped like a W. Cepheus is on one side of Cassiopeia, and Andromeda is on the other. Pegasus can be spotted above Andromeda, while Perseus is below it.

CEPHEUS

*CEPHEUS AND CASSIOPEIA, SHOWN HERE, CAN BE SEEN IN THE SKY ALL YEAR IN THE NORTHERN HEMISPHERE, BUT THE ENTIRE PERSEUS FAMILY IS BEST SEEN IN FALL.*

CASSIOPEIA

## STAR STORY

Cetus is also known as the Whale, Triangulum is also called the Triangle, and Lacerta is the Lizard. These other names can help you figure out the shapes of these constellations.

# NAMING THE STARS

Some of the brightest stars in Andromeda have names that can be traced back to the Arabic language. This was the language used by people who studied the stars thousands of years ago in the Middle East.

Alpheratz, which is the brightest star in Andromeda, is also called Sirrah. Both of these names are Arabic words that mean "horse's navel." Another star in Andromeda, Mirach, has a name that means "the **loins**" in Arabic. The star Almach, which can also be spelled Almaak, got its name from the Arabic word for a weasel-like animal.

**STAR STORY**
The name "horse's navel" comes from the fact that Arabian stargazers thought of Alpheratz as part of Pegasus, the flying horse. A horse's navel is its belly button!

STARGAZERS FROM THE MIDDLE EAST PLAYED AN IMPORTANT PART IN THE HISTORY OF ASTRONOMY, OR THE STUDY OF SPACE.

# NEW NAMES

Every star in Andromeda has a name—not just the brightest ones. In fact, every star in each of the 88 constellations has a name. One system of naming stars was created in 1603 by German astronomer Johann Bayer. He assigned each star in a constellation a letter from the Greek alphabet. That letter was then added to the **Latin** spelling of the constellation's name.

For example, Alpheratz is called "Alpha Andromedae" because Alpha is the first letter in the Greek alphabet, and Alpheratz is the brightest star in Andromeda. "Andromedae" is the way "Andromeda" is spelled in Latin.

**STAR STORY**
British astronomer John Flamsteed introduced a new naming system for stars in 1725, using numbers and Latin names to **identify** stars in constellations.

ALPHA ANDROMEDAE

IF YOU SEE THE BRIGHTEST STAR IN ANDROMEDA AND THE GREAT SQUARE OF PEGASUS, YOU'VE FOUND ALPHA ANDROMEDAE!

# WHAT'S M31?

Astronomers study the night sky with tools called telescopes, which use lenses and mirrors to make faraway space objects appear larger. In the 1700s, French astronomer Charles Messier used telescopes to search for **comets**. While searching, he found many other unknown objects in the sky.

In 1760, Messier began writing down a catalog, or list, of the objects he found that were different from comets. Messier and the people he worked with listed a total of 110 star clusters, galaxies, and nebulae, which are clouds of gas and dust in space. One of the galaxies they discovered is found in the Andromeda constellation. It's known as the Andromeda Galaxy.

**STAR STORY**
A galaxy is any one of the very large groups of stars that make up the **universe**.

MESSIER NUMBERED THE OBJECTS IN THE ORDER IN WHICH HE FOUND THEM. THE ANDROMEDA GALAXY, SHOWN HERE, IS ALSO KNOWN AS M31.

# SPIRAL GALAXIES

A galaxy is held together by gravity, which is the natural force that causes stars and planets to move toward each other. Our **solar system** is part of a galaxy called the Milky Way. The Andromeda and the Milky Way Galaxies are just two of over 100 billion galaxies in the universe.

SCIENTISTS BELIEVE THAT THE ANDROMEDA AND THE MILKY WAY GALAXIES WILL COLLIDE BILLIONS OF YEARS FROM NOW. THIS IS A PICTURE OF WHAT IT MIGHT LOOK LIKE WHEN THEY COLLIDE.

MILKY WAY GALAXY

ANDROMEDA GALAXY

Both the Andromeda and the Milky Way Galaxies are spiral galaxies. A spiral galaxy looks like a pinwheel when seen from above. From the side, it looks like a flat disk with a ball stuck in the center. The Andromeda Galaxy can be seen in the night sky.

**STAR STORY**
The Andromeda Galaxy can be seen without a telescope. It looks like a large **smudge** in the sky near the Andromeda constellation.

# A GIANT GALAXY

The Andromeda Galaxy may be the closest galaxy to the Milky Way, but it's still very far away. It's 2.5 million light-years from Earth. What's a light-year? It's a unit that equals the distance light can travel in one year. One light-year is around 5.9 trillion miles (9.5 trillion km).

The Andromeda Galaxy was once known as a nebula, but when astronomers discovered how big it really is, they renamed it a galaxy. The Andromeda Galaxy is more than 200,000 light-years across, while the Milky Way is only about 100,000 light-years across.

**STAR STORY**

Andromeda was named a galaxy in the 1920s by the American astronomer Edwin Powell Hubble.

ANDROMEDA

CASSIOPEIA

ANDROMEDA GALAXY
M31

IN ORDER TO FIND THE ANDROMEDA GALAXY IN THE NIGHT SKY, LOOK FOR THE CONSTELLATIONS ANDROMEDA AND CASSIOPEIA. THE GALAXY CAN BE SEEN BETWEEN THEM, WITH ONE OF THE POINTS IN CASSIOPEIA'S W SHAPE POINTING TO THE GALAXY LIKE AN ARROW!

# SEARCHING THE STARS

Andromeda is an important constellation because it helps people find the Andromeda Galaxy. Scientists study the Andromeda Galaxy to learn more about the universe and about our own Milky Way Galaxy. Both galaxies are part of a group of galaxies known as the Local Group. The Local Group includes 30 galaxies that are close to Earth.

The next time you go outside at night, look up at the stars and see if you can find the stars that make up Andromeda. You might even be able to see the Andromeda Galaxy, too!

# GLOSSARY

**comet:** An object in outer space made mostly of ice and dust that often develops one or more long tails when near the sun.

**hemisphere:** Half of Earth.

**identify:** To find out or show what something is.

**Latin:** The language of ancient Rome.

**loin:** An area on the back and sides of an animal's body near the tail.

**mythology:** A set of stories told in ancient cultures to explain a practice, belief, or part of nature.

**nymph:** A spirit in the shape of a young woman.

**smudge:** A blurry spot or streak.

**solar system:** The sun and space objects that travel around it.

**universe:** Everything that exists.

# INDEX

# WEBSITES

Due to the changing nature of Internet links, PowerKids Press has developed an online list of websites related to the subject of this book. This site is updated regularly. Please use this link to access the list: www.powerkidslinks.com/tcc/and